TONY EVANS
SPEAKS OUT ON
PRAYER

TONY EVANS
SPEAKS OUT ON
PRAYER

MOODY PRESS
CHICAGO

Scripture quotations are taken from the *New American Standard Bible*®, © Copyright The Lockman Foundation 1960, 1962, 1963, 1968, 1971, 1972, 1973, 1975, 1977, 1995. Used by permission.

ISBN: 0-8024-4368-0

1 3 5 7 9 10 8 6 4 2

Printed in the United States of America

PRAYER

My normal method of driving is with my car's gas tank as near empty as possible. I stop at a gas station only as a last resort. Anytime my wife, Lois, has to drive my car, she first asks if there is anything in the tank because she knows I drive on fumes.

One reason I do this is that I've gotten away with it so often. I can't tell you how many times I've pulled into the gas station just in the nick of time.

One time when Lois was with me in the car, she was telling me I was going to get in trouble someday driving around with an empty gas tank. Sure enough, the car started to cough and run out of gas, but I was able to exit the highway on a downhill ramp, and there was a gas station at the bottom.

So I said to Lois, "See what happens when you know Jesus?"

Well, I wasn't as fortunate the next time my car ran

out of gas. I wound up stranded on the side of the road, standing by my car feeling very embarrassed.

Take it from me. You won't get very far driving around on gas fumes. That's a very powerless, frustrating way to travel.

A lot of Christians are trying to operate their spiritual lives the way I drive my car. They are running on fumes—trying to get somewhere for the Lord without using the fuel that provides the spark that energizes the power of God resident within us through the Holy Spirit.

The fuel that provides the spiritual spark is *prayer*. You can't get very far in the walk of faith without a prayer life, yet many Christians are doing it because they think they're getting away with it. They're like me in my car, ignoring their need to pray until their tanks go empty and they wind up on the side of the road looking for help.

Many of us struggle with the spiritual discipline of prayer. Some believers know how much they need to cultivate a prayer life as a vital part of their daily lives. To others, prayer is more like the national anthem at a ball game. It gets the game started, but it is not seen as having anything to do with the action on the field.

It helps to know we are not the first people to struggle with prayer. Jesus' disciples watched Him pray one day and said, "Lord, teach us to pray" (Luke 11:1).

That's interesting because they didn't ask Jesus to teach them how to preach. But when the disciples watched Jesus pray, and saw the intimacy between the

Son and the Father and what the Father did for the Son, they said, "We need to get in on this."

Jesus answered the disciples' request by offering a model prayer we call the Lord's Prayer. That's actually a misnomer, because this is not a prayer Jesus would pray. Jesus had no "debts" or sins to be forgiven.

This is really the disciples' prayer. Jesus didn't mean this was the only prayer we are to use, or that we need to pray these exact words. The Lord's Prayer is a marvelous example, an outline, of how to pray. It gives us a pattern for prayer.

THE PARAMETERS OF PRAYER

Before we begin a detailed study of this amazing prayer, let me give you a basic definition of prayer. *Prayer is a believer's communication with God the Father, through the authority and Person of Jesus Christ, assisted by the Holy Spirit.* Let's break this down.

The key word is communication, not just talking. God is a Person to be communicated with, not someone for us to talk at. The test of prayer is whether God is the audience of your conversation.

Our prayer is to be offered through Jesus Christ. The only reason you and I have access to God is that the door was opened by the blood of Christ. Jesus said, "I am the way, and the truth, and the life; no one comes to the Father but through Me" (John 14:6).

We can't come into the presence of a holy God unless we are escorted by the Son. That's why we pray in Jesus' name. That's not a nice religious tag to tack on to the end of our prayers. Jesus is our access to God, and because of what Jesus did on the cross we can "draw near with confidence to the throne of grace" (Hebrews 4:16).

Prayer is also assisted by the Holy Spirit. Romans 8:26–27 says the Holy Spirit helps us in our prayers because we are weak and don't always know how to pray as we ought. Sometimes we don't know what to say, and other times we're hurting too much to say anything.

But look what the Holy Spirit does for us. "The Spirit Himself intercedes for us with groanings too deep for words" (v. 26b). When all we can do is groan and grope for the right words, the Spirit interprets those expressions and turns them into intelligible requests before the Father. The Spirit knows what we mean even when we don't know what we mean.

In other words, the Holy Spirit's ministry in prayer is to take what cannot be clarified and clarify it. That's why you're not wasting your time praying even when you don't know what to say, because the Spirit is at work organizing your confusion.

True prayer is limited to the sphere of the Trinity—but that means the parameters of prayer are limitless because we are talking about the infinite God.

THE PRECAUTIONS OF PRAYER

The Lord's Prayer is set in what I call a precautionary context. That's because before Jesus gave His disciples their model for prayer, He taught several important principles about prayer that we need to consider.

The first principle is that we need to pray *regularly*. Jesus said, "*When* you pray" (Matthew 6:5, italics added). Notice He didn't say "If you pray," or "It's up to you whether you pray." Our need to pray is the unstated assumption behind Jesus' statement.

Prayer must be a regular part of our lives because it's such a critical part of our lives. One reason prayer is so important is that it is an expression of faith, and the Bible says, "Without faith it is impossible to please [God]" (Hebrews 11:6).

Jesus also said we need to pray *sincerely*.

When you pray, you are not to be like the hypocrites; for they love to stand and pray in the synagogues and on the street corners so that they may be seen by men. Truly I say to you, they have their reward in full. (Matthew 6:5)

This takes us back to verse 1, where Jesus said, "Beware of practicing your righteousness before men to be noticed by them; otherwise you have no reward with your Father who is in heaven."

Most of the Jews in Jesus' day prayed three times a day. The hypocrites who prayed only to be seen and heard by others went to the most crowded, public places to pray.

They were like the little boy whose grandmother was visiting. He was praying in his bedroom one night while his mother and grandmother were sitting in the living room. His mother heard him say very loudly, "And Lord, please give me a bicycle for Christmas."

She went into the bedroom and said, "Son, you don't have to yell. God can hear you."

"I know, Mom," the boy answered. "But Grandma can't hear very well, and she's got the money to buy me a bike."

How do you measure sincerity in prayer? Jesus told us, "When you pray, go into your inner room, close your door and pray to your Father who is in secret, and your Father who sees what is done in secret will reward you" (Matthew 6:6). We must pray *secretly.*

Jesus wasn't just equating being alone with effective prayer. Praying in secret means refusing to make a show out of prayer. It means shutting out anything and everything that keeps you from concentrating on God. A closed door refers to an undistracted environment for prayer.

Obviously, shutting yourself off from other people and distractions is one way to achieve secrecy in prayer. This is crucial because it doesn't take much to drown out God's voice. God is a spirit, so if you are going to connect with Him you must connect spiritually.

When God sees that you want to be in His presence so much you're willing to remove all distractions— when He sees you in secret and knows you are not playing to the crowd—then He shows up.

God also wants us to pray *thoughtfully.* "And when you are praying, do not use meaningless repetition as the Gentiles do, for they suppose that they will be heard for their many words" (Matthew 6:7). "Meaningless repetition" means babble, and babble means thoughtless verbiage, saying the same words without any thought behind them.

If I asked you for your home address, you could probably rattle it off without even stopping to think about it. You've given out your address so many times you have it down cold. That's the way some people pray.

I remember when I was a boy, if my mother had fried chicken for dinner and it was my turn to pray, I prayed with my eyes open and my hands on the far side of my plate. That way, I was ready to grab the piece of chicken I wanted.

I can tell you, I wasn't thinking about God. My mind was on that fried chicken. I just had to get past the prayer to get it.

Sometimes, prayer is just words we toss out to salute God so we can get on to the real deal. *Hurry up and pray so we can start the meeting and get to the real issues.*

The best way to avoid meaningless repetition is to continue getting to know God. The better you know a person, the more the two of you have to discuss. Whenever you learn something new about our great God, include that in your prayer life.

Jesus added, "So do not be like them; for your Father knows what you need before you ask Him" (Matthew 6:8). You don't have to inform God of anything in prayer. As a good Father, He already knows all about you, including what you need.

PRIORITY ONE: GOD'S WILL

When we begin to understand how vital it is to pray regularly, sincerely, secretly, and thoughtfully, we are ready to learn more about how to pray. That was the next subject Jesus addressed with the disciples as He taught the Lord's Prayer.

Let's go through this great prayer phrase by phrase as we seek to understand what Jesus is teaching us about prayer.

The Paternity of Prayer

You probably know the first two words of the Lord's Prayer. This is a child addressing a loving Father. Jesus said, "Pray, then, in this way: 'Our Father who is in heaven, hallowed be Your name'" (Matthew 6:9).

Notice this is "Our Father," not "My Father." You're not an only child in this family. The Father wants us to know that when we come to Him other siblings are involved. We can't be selfish in prayer.

Since only believers can pray and expect God to hear, "Our Father" means God is not everybody's Father. Jesus said to the unbelieving religious leaders of His day, "You are of your father the devil" (John 8:44). Only those who receive Christ as Savior and are born from above are given the right to be called the children of God (John 1:12).

The fact that all believers are invited to pray to the

Father means all of us have equal access to God. He doesn't have favorite kids. If you're in the family of God, you bear His name and have full access to the Father.

Let me tell you some wonderful things about the heavenly Father to whom we pray. When you have a real father who loves you and cares for you and protects you and disciplines you, you have somebody you can trust. Your welfare is always on his mind. In fact, you can trust a loving father's heart even when you can't figure why he's doing what he's doing.

Being able to say "Our Father" also addresses the problem of worry. Later in Matthew 6, Jesus talked about worry (vv. 25–34). He said don't worry about having enough food or water or clothes. In fact, it's a sin to worry because Jesus commanded us not to do it (v. 34).

You say, "I'm not worried, Tony. I'm just concerned."

Well, if your concern is keeping you up at night, it's a worry. If your concern is ruining your health, it's a worry. If your concern keeps you constantly depressed, it's a worry. And it's sin.

What's the cure for worry? Knowing and trusting your Father. "Your heavenly Father knows that you need all these things. But seek first His kingdom and His righteousness; and all these things will be added to to you" (Matthew 6:32–33).

Jesus said His Father even takes care of the birds (v. 26). Have you ever seen a worried bird? Do birds get high blood pressure or bad nerves from worry? No, they just go out each day knowing there's going to be a worm or a seed somewhere. Having a Father who cares means you don't have to worry.

It also means you don't have to be afraid, even in the most difficult circumstances or the darkest hour. Those may be the times when you don't know what your heavenly Father is doing in your life, but since you know He has your welfare at heart, you can conquer the fear the Enemy throws at you.

If God is your Father, He's also in charge. He makes the final decisions. You can make your request and tell Him what you want, and sometimes He will say yes. But because God is dealing with His whole family and not just one child, sometimes He will say no for His greater purpose. He has that prerogative as our Father.

Praying "Our Father" means we accept His right to discipline us too. Every good father disciplines his children, and God disciplines His own (Hebrews 12:4–11).

Let me give you one other benefit that comes to those who can legitimately pray, "Our Father." This statement of intimacy means availability.

No matter how many meetings I may have at church, no matter what I may be doing, my children can always get through to me if they need me. My assistant, Sylvia, knows that whenever the kids call, she can go ahead and put them through. I may not be able to talk to them very long, but I want them to know that my work at church doesn't get in the way of my being a father.

Let me tell you some good news. Being Ruler of the universe doesn't get in the way of God's being our Father!

After saying "Our Father," we are taught to say, "Who is in heaven." Why do we need to be reminded in prayer that God our Father is in heaven? Because it tells us He is not subject to the limitations of earth. Earth does not have the final say-so in our lives. God rules from heaven, so He can do anything He wants to do on our behalf.

Jesus taught us to say to this Father who rules from heaven, "Hallowed be Your name." The word "hallowed" is from the same root as the word "holy." It means to set something or someone apart as unique or special. When we pray this way, we are saying, "God, I recognize that You are in a class by Yourself. You alone are holy."

The name of God deserves to be hallowed because God's name is the sum total of His attributes. In the Bible, a person's name reflects that person's character.

If you know your Bible, you know that God has many names. Each name addresses a different aspect of His perfect character, and each one also speaks to any situation we might find ourselves in or any need we might have.

Not all of these names are readily obvious in the English text of the Bible, so let me give you the Hebrew word or words, their translation, and what they mean. Here are some of the names for God in the Bible.

In Genesis 1:1, God is called *Elohim.* "In the beginning, Elohim . . ." This is a plural word that emphasizes God's majesty, power, and glory. *Elohim* is the mighty Creator God who can speak worlds into existence and meet you in your weakness.

God is also *El Elyon,* "God Most High." This name means He's the God who is high and exalted and can do great things. David wrote, "I will cry to God Most High, to God who accomplishes all things for me" (Psalm 57:2). When everything in your life is out of order and disjointed, you need to know *El Elyon.*

In Psalm 91:1, the psalmist urges us to "abide in the shadow of the Almighty," *El Shaddai,* a name for God that speaks of His strength. Even when you have no strength, you have not exhausted your resources because God says, "My name is *El Shaddai.*"

Another wonderful name for God comes from an unlikely source. Sarah's Egyptian maid Hagar, who bore Ishmael to Abraham, was thrown out of the house by Sarah. Hagar thought she was finished, but God came to her and promised her a heritage through Ishmael. Hagar responded by calling God *El Roi,* "God who sees" (Genesis 16:13). Even when you feel like you're alone and have no hope, God sees you. He hasn't forgotten you.

God is called *El Olam,* "the Everlasting God" (Genesis 21:33) who is in no hurry and will take the time to do what is best for us.

There are so many more names for God in the Bible, and each one has a special meaning and holds special hope for us. Let me give you a few more examples.

Jehovah is the most sacred name of God, which speaks of His self-existence. "I AM WHO I AM," God told Moses (Exodus 3:14). *Jehovah* needs no assistance. This name was often paired with other words for even more emphasis on part of God's character.

He is *Jehovah-shalom,* "the Lord is Peace" (Judges 6:24), the only source of lasting peace. God is also *Jehovah-nissi,* "the Lord is My Banner" (Exodus 17:15). The banner was raised as a rallying point for an army going into battle. It was a symbol of victory.

We're talking about the name of God, which Jesus said is to be hallowed. One way to avoid meaningless repetition is to think about the awesome names of the God to whom we pray. There are so many more names.

The Lord is *Jehovah-raah,* our Shepherd and Provider (Psalm 23:1) and *Jehovah-rapha,* the Lord our healer (Exodus 15:26), meaning you're never alone. And when we sin, God is *Jehovah-tsidkenu,* "the Lord our righteousness" (Jeremiah 23:6), who covers us with His righteousness. And when we have a need, God is *Jehovah-jireh,* "the Lord Will Provide" (Genesis 22:14).

Your Father in heaven is in charge.

This is the God who teaches us to call Him "Our Father."

You don't need to know Hebrew to know God. When you pray "Our Father," you just need to know that He is everything you will ever need.

The Program of Prayer

The next sentence in the Lord's Prayer is the first request made of God, which is "Your kingdom come" (Matthew 6:10a). Once we get God's person in focus, then we must connect with His program.

That is a simple request to make, but let me show you what it means for us to pray that God's kingdom will come. When we were born again by faith in Jesus Christ, we became citizens of God's kingdom.

The word *kingdom* means rule or authority. So when we talk about God's kingdom, we are talking about His comprehensive rule over all of His creation. The Bible is very clear that God holds ultimate authority. "The Lord has established His throne in the heavens, and His sovereignty rules over all" (Psalm 103:19).

Your Father in heaven is in charge. So when you pray, you are not coming to some anemic ruler who is powerless to help you. God is sovereign over all.

But if God is the sovereign Ruler of His kingdom, that places some demands on us. In other words, we cannot hallow God's name if we are not willing to serve His kingdom. We can't pray, "Our Father who is in heaven, hallowed be Your name," and then say, "Now let's discuss my program on earth." When it comes to the kingdom program, heaven informs and rules over earth, not vice versa.

King Belshazzar of Babylon, the grandson of Nebuchadnezzar, learned that lesson the hard way. Belshazzar thought he could mock God during a drunken orgy, but a hand appeared and wrote the king's doom on a wall. Belshazzar panicked and called in the prophet Daniel.

Daniel reminded Belshazzar that Nebuchadnezzar had been driven mad "until he recognized that the Most High God is ruler over the realm of mankind and that He sets over it whomever He wishes" (Daniel 5:21). Then Daniel said, "Yet you, his son, Belshazzar, have not humbled your heart, even though you knew all this" (v. 22).

Daniel 5:23–31 tells the rest of the story, including the famous handwriting on the wall and the fall of Belshazzar's kingdom that same night. God will not allow any earthly kingdom to impose its rule over His heavenly kingdom.

It's important to remember that God's kingdom is spiritual at its source. Pontius Pilate asked Jesus, "Are You the King of the Jews?" (John 18:33).

Jesus answered, "My kingdom is not of this world. If My kingdom were of this world, then My servants would be fighting so that I would not be handed over to the Jews; but as it is, My kingdom is not of this realm" (v. 36).

Jesus was saying His kingdom is from the spiritual realm. That's why prayer is so important. It transports you to another realm above and outside of the physical realm, the world of the five senses. God's kingdom is invisible—although when Christ returns the kingdom will be made gloriously visible for a thousand years.

But for us today, learning to pray according to the pattern Jesus taught us, the kingdom of God is invisible. So when we pray for the kingdom to come, we are asking God to make His invisible kingdom visible in our experience.

But in order for this to happen, God's program must be the preoccupation of our lives. You can't pray "Your kingdom come" and then come to God only when you want something to enhance your program. That's not what prayer is all about. You don't get God's benefits and blessings without submitting yourself to His kingdom rule.

What are we praying for when we pray for God's kingdom to come? We are asking God to manifest His power. Before Jesus' ascension, the disciples asked, "Lord, is it at this time You are restoring the kingdom to Israel?" (Acts 1:6).

Jesus told them not to worry about when He was coming back, because the immediate issue was the progress of God's kingdom program in their lives. "You will receive power when the Holy Spirit has come upon you" (v. 8). Jesus was saying, "You will have to wait for Me to come back, but you will not have to wait for My power."

God's power is made available to us so we can make the kingdom proclamation that He is Savior and Lord. Jesus went on to say in Acts 1:8, "You shall be My witnesses."

Now this raises a question. If we have all the power of God available to us to carry out His plan of proclaiming the kingdom, why are so many Christians so powerless, and why don't we witness more than we do? Why aren't we proclaiming the King?

The answer is that we are so detached from God's kingdom program that we don't really want to talk about His Person. According to 1 Peter 2:9, we are designed to be a kingdom of priests proclaiming the excellencies of Christ. If we're not excited about seeing God's kingdom made manifest in power, then we're not going to get too worked up about proclaiming the excellencies of our glorious Lord and King.

That's tragic, because God's kingdom comes with a glorious Prince. The prophet wrote,

> A child will be born to us, a son will be given to us; and the government will rest on His shoulders; and His name will be called Wonderful Counselor, Mighty God, Eternal Father, Prince of Peace. There will be no end to the increase of His government or of peace. (Isaiah 9:6–7)

That's a prophecy of Jesus Christ in His first coming as the Child of Bethlehem and His second coming as Prince of Peace who will rule God's kingdom. Isaiah said there would be no limit to the increase of His rule and His peace.

As we said, Christ will rule on earth when He comes back, but because His kingdom is spiritual and eternal we can experience His peace and His rule in our hearts today.

But notice that those two things go together. If we want God's peace, we must accept His rule. And the more peace we want, the more His rule must increase in our lives. When we are ready to enact God's program, His government, we will enjoy His kingdom peace.

The Priority of Prayer

The next principle of prayer that Jesus taught in the model prayer of Matthew 6 is this: "Your will be done, on earth as it is in heaven" (v. 10b).

If we are going to bow to the rule of God's kingdom program, it makes sense that we will want what God wants, when He wants it, and the way He wants it. That's a basic definition of God's will, which is His priority for us.

But bowing to God's will is a struggle for many believers, for the reason we mentioned above. We spend too much time asking God to rubber-stamp our program and our plan. But let me point out that we are halfway through the Lord's Prayer and our requests haven't even come up yet. Those don't start until verse 11. God's Person, His program, and His priority come first.

What are we asking for when we pray that God's will would be done? There are three basic aspects of God's will.

The first is God's comprehensive will, His overarching plan for His creation. This means that nothing catches God by surprise. He never has to say, "Did you see that? I didn't know that was going to happen."

God also has what we could call His compassionate will. This includes His stated desires, which may or may not come to pass.

For instance, God's will is that all people be saved (2 Peter 3:9), although it is obvious that not everybody is saved. Jesus said of Jerusalem, "How often I wanted to gather your children together . . . and you would not have it!" (Luke 13:34). The reason God's compassionate will does not always come to pass is that He allows human beings a choice.

Don't misunderstand. No choice by a human being or the devil himself will slow God down at all or hinder Him in any way in accomplishing whatever He wants to accomplish. That's good news because it means other people can't stop the will of God for you and the devil can't stop the will of God for you.

The third facet of God's will is His commanded will. These are specific things God has commanded to enable us to be the full beneficiaries of His program. For instance, Paul said that God's stated will for us is to avoid sexual immorality (1 Thessalonians 4:3).

Romans 12:1–2 is the most comprehensive statement of God's will for His people:

> Therefore I urge you, brethren, by the mercies of God, to present your bodies a living and holy sacrifice, acceptable to God, which is your spiritual service of worship. And do not be conformed to this world, but be transformed by the renewing of your mind, so that you may prove what the will of God is, that which is good and acceptable and perfect.

God's will is flawless, perfect in every detail (see 2 Samuel 22:31). So when we pray for His will to be carried out on earth, we are asking for an awesome force to be unleashed.

Let me say a word about what should happen when we come into conflict with God's will. The mere fact we have to pray "Your will be done" means it is possible for us not to do it. Jesus taught us to pray this way because our human will often clashes with God's perfect will.

Why do we sometimes oppose God's will, even as believers? One reason is that we're not really sure we can trust God. We are saying to God, in effect, "Lord, I'm not sure if I do this Your way that it's going to come out for the best. I'm afraid to trust you with my life."

Another time we conflict with God's will is when we want to go our sinful way no matter what God says. What we want to do looks good, tastes good, and feels good. It's what we want the way we want it when we want it—the exact opposite of God's will.

What is God's concern in our praying? This is stated in the last half of Matthew 6:10. God's concern is that His will be done "on earth as it is in heaven." We need to see how God's will is done in heaven so we can do it the same way on earth.

First, God's will is done immediately in heaven. When the prophet Isaiah had his great vision of God, he saw seraphim with six wings, two of which they used for flying (Isaiah 6:1–2). The picture here is of swiftness, angelic beings ready to obey God's command in an instant.

God's will is also carried out fully and perfectly in heaven. There is no debate or discussion in heaven about God's will. The only person who ever debated God doesn't live there anymore. In heaven, there is full conformity to the will of God.

God's will is also done absolutely in heaven. There is no other being in heaven with a will that is independent of God or in conflict with Him.

Jesus is our great example here, because He never failed to do what His Father wanted, even when it meant the cross. Jesus' prayer in the Garden of Gethsemane is our model: "Your will be done" (Matthew 26:42). Prayer is a means of getting heaven's will done on earth, not getting earth's will done in heaven.

So what's the payoff for doing God's will? That is given to us in the last half of the Lord's Prayer, when it comes to praying for our needs (Matthew 6:11–13).

For example, when you do God's will you get to pray for His daily bread, His forgiveness for your sins, and His deliverance from temptation. But when you do your will, you get to find your own bread, you have to deal with your own sins, and you must try to protect yourself from the devil's attacks.

The apostle John wrote,

This is the confidence which we have before Him, that, if we ask anything according to His will, He hears us. And if we know that He hears us in whatever we ask, we know that we have the requests which we have asked from Him. (1 John 5:14–15)

John is saying that if you are willing to say to God, "Your will be done," and really mean it regardless of what you may want, then your prayers are going to get ears opened in heaven. Jesus said in John 12:26 that whoever serves Him will be honored by His Father.

I hope you know that doing God's will doesn't mean a problem-free existence. It doesn't mean the absence of tests.

Jesus once ordered His disciples to cross the sea, which took them straight into the middle of a storm on the Sea of Galilee (Mark 4:35–41). They were terrified, while He slept on a cushion. The storm was a test to see if they would obey His will and trust Him even when it looked bad. They were in the storm, but they had Jesus with them.

The question is, Do you trust God's will even when He puts you in the storm? If so, you'll experience His presence to calm the storm.

PRIORITY TWO: THE PROVISION OF PRAYER

Now we're ready to address the second half of Jesus' model prayer, the verses in which we make our needs and requests known to our heavenly Father.

Jesus taught us to pray, "Give us this day our daily bread" (Matthew 6:11). One reason we are to ask our heavenly Father for our food is that we don't want the wrong person feeding us.

Did you know that the devil has a food program? He does, and he offered it to Jesus in the wilderness temptation (Matthew 4:3) just before Jesus gave the Sermon on the Mount.

Satan tempted Jesus to turn stones into bread, but Jesus refused because the bread would have been from the wrong source. It's more important where your daily bread comes from than whether you have enough bread.

As the Israelites were ready to enter Canaan, God warned them, "Beware that you do not forget the Lord your God" (Deuteronomy 8:11).

Why were the Israelites in danger of forgetting God? Because they were going into a good land, and if they weren't careful they would forget that God gave it to them. Then they would start saying, "My power and the strength of my hand made me this wealth" (v. 17).

We can do the same thing. We can forget God and get the big head and start saying, "Wait a minute. I'm the one making the living here. I built this company with my own hands. I'm the one making the great deals. I've earned everything I have by my own hard work and dedication."

God has a remedy for that kind of spiritual amnesia. "You shall remember the Lord your God, for it is He who is giving you power to make wealth" (Deuteronomy 8:18).

How does God give you the strength to make a living? By providing the bread you have to eat before you can even go to work. Whatever you eat comes from something God has made. Asking God for your daily bread is a great reminder of who your Provider really is.

Jesus used bread here to represent all of our physical needs. He was saying that if we are taking care of God's priorities and concerns, we won't have to worry about our bread. If we are serving God's kingdom, the King will cover our needs.

But what we do so often is let our physical needs get ahead of our spiritual priorities, and we wind up messed up on both counts. When you make bread an end in itself, then your only concern is, "When do we eat?" You don't care too much who provided the bread.

Jesus' example in the wilderness teaches us that God is more important than our physical satisfaction. When we find our satisfaction and sustenance in Him, then the promise of Philippians 4:19 kicks in. "My God will supply all your needs according to His riches in glory in Christ Jesus."

Notice that Paul said "according to," not "out of." A wealthy person could give you a measly dollar out of his riches. But if he were to give you a gift according to, or in keeping with, his riches, you'd have something special coming.

Recently, I was talking to a businessman who was trying to close a million-dollar deal. He wanted me to pray with him about this deal. I said, "Before we pray, let me ask you a question. If this deal goes through, what does God get out of it?"

He started scratching his head and rubbing his eyes because he had not considered that before. You see, when you start praying, "Give me," and God isn't part of the deal, you've got it backwards.

God has promised to supply our needs when we are putting Him and His kingdom first (see Matthew 6:33). But there are times when He may not do that. I can think of two situations.

The first is suggested by the conversation I had with that businessman. That is, God may not meet our needs because of our carnality. Like the prodigal son, we may be in a far country eating with the pigs when God is abundantly supplying everyone's needs back home in the Father's house. When we get up and come back home, God will start meeting our needs.

Jesus emphasized the "dailyness" of God's supply.

Another occasion when God may not meet our physical needs is when He is testing us to take us to the next spiritual level. The issue here is not whether God will meet a need, but when.

God may have a specific purpose for not responding immediately, but David could say confidently, "I have been young and now I am old, yet I have not seen the righteous forsaken or his descendants begging bread" (Psalm 37:25). God the Father has never walked out on His children.

This is also a selfless prayer: "Give *us* this day our

daily bread." In other words, you cannot be concerned only about your needs in prayer. You can't say, "Lord, I don't care if other folk are starving. Feed me." Prayer that never gets beyond me and my needs is not something God can bless.

The provision we are taught to pray for is supplied "this day." Jesus emphasized the "dailyness" of God's supply.

The best example of this is Israel in the wilderness. The people were hungry, so God rained down a white, flaky substance called manna (Exodus 16:13–21). Manna was bread from heaven, and God's instruction was that the Israelites were only to gather enough for each day. Anything they tried to keep overnight, except for the Sabbath, turned rancid or stale.

A lot of us are living off of stale blessings. We haven't hallowed God's name, prioritized His kingdom, or obeyed His will, so by the time we get to our bread, it's stale. Nobody wants stale bread. We want it to be fresh. But we can't enjoy it fresh when we are giving God our stale, leftover service.

Why does God want us to come to Him each day for our needs? Because coming keeps us thankful and dependent. When the refrigerator and freezer are full, it's easy to forget to trust God and not depend on His provision. We need this truth in our culture because most of us have tomorrow's food on hand today.

I strongly suggest that you fast once in a while as a family, just to remind you where your daily bread comes from and what it feels like not to have it. Fasting wouldn't hurt most of us, because we're an overeating generation. The issue is not just going hungry for a meal or a day. The issue is learning how dependent we are on God and reminding ourselves daily that He alone is our Source. What we say about our pets, God says about us: "Don't bite the hand that feeds you."

The Pardon of Prayer

The next request in the Lord's Prayer is also crucial. "And forgive us our debts, as we also have forgiven our debtors" (Matthew 6:12).

Here Jesus introduced us to the very difficult subject of forgiveness. There is probably not a person reading this page who has not struggled with forgiveness.

The issue of forgiveness is real because the problem of sin is real. When we sin, or someone sins against us, it's like a person running up a bill or accumulating a debt. There is something real that needs to be addressed.

The word *forgive* means "to hurl away." Forgiveness has to do with casting or throwing away that which has caused the problem—in this case, the sin that blocks our relationship with God and with others.

Forgiveness, then, is the decision to no longer carry an offense on the books, not to keep the offender in debt. Forgiveness means to cancel the debt and release the debtor. The opposite of this would be the refusal to let go of the debt, or to retaliate against the sinner.

Now the fact that Jesus taught His disciples to pray this way raises a theological question. This is a prayer believers are to pray. But you may say, "I thought that as a Christian, I was already forgiven. Why do I need to pursue forgiveness?"

The answer is that the Bible teaches two kinds of forgiveness. There is the judicial or legal forgiveness we received when we trusted Christ. In the courtroom of heaven, our sin debt was paid and our sin account was closed. When God forgave you, He took care of your sins past, present, and future, so that your sins will never come up again before God with regard to your standing before Him.

The second kind of forgiveness is relational forgiveness. This is the forgiveness we are urged to pursue in 1 John 1:9, cleansing from the effects of our sin that cause a break in our fellowship and intimacy with our heavenly Father. God doesn't deal with His children as a Judge, but as our Father. Although the legal issue of sin is settled once for all, the relational issue of sin has to be dealt with regularly.

We do this with our children. Legally, they belong to us even on their worst days. But that doesn't mean they are always in good relational standing with us. When they mess up, we forgive them and restore the closeness. In the Lord's Prayer we are asking God to remove the barrier our sins have erected between Him and us, and restore us to the joy of His favor.

This raises the question of the relationship between forgiving and forgetting. Does God forget our sins once He has forgiven them?

The Bible says so. God told His people, "I will not remember your sins" (Isaiah 43:25). That doesn't mean God is no longer able to recall what we did. If that were true, He could not be omniscient.

What God does is let go of our sins so they no longer count against us. A good example might be a very high bell tower with a rope attached to the bell. Forgiveness is cutting the rope.

The criterion of forgiveness is also given in Matthew 6:12: "Forgive us our debts, as we also have forgiven our debtors." We must be willing to grant others what we ourselves expect from God. To ask God to forgive you when you won't forgive somebody else is to destroy the bridge over which you yourself must cross.

Evidently, forgiveness was the most important theme of the Lord's Prayer, because it's the only part of the prayer that Jesus gave further comment on: "For if you forgive others for their transgressions, your heavenly Father will also forgive you. But if you do not forgive others, then your Father will not forgive your transgressions" (vv. 14–15).

One reason this is so crucial is because of what it cost God to forgive us. Giving His only Son to die for us was a very expensive provision, so He does not want us to take our responsibility to forgive lightly.

There are two ways you can forgive others. The first is to forgive unilaterally. By that I mean forgiving another person when your forgiveness has not been sought.

There are several examples of this in the Bible. As Stephen was being stoned to death, he prayed, "Lord, do not hold this sin against them!" (Acts 7:60).

But the greatest example of unilateral forgiveness was Jesus as He was being crucified. He prayed, "Father, forgive them; for they do not know what they are doing" (Luke 23:34).

The second form of forgiveness is transactional forgiveness. This is when both parties are involved, when the offender seeks forgiveness and receives it. Transactional forgiveness involves an exchange, and is based on repentance.

How do you know when the person who asks for forgiveness is truly repentant? You can't see into a person's heart, but you can watch someone's actions and look for the fruit of repentance. A person who is seeking forgiveness and is truly repentant will manifest that repentance in actions that help heal the wound.

What happens when we fail to forgive others the way God has forgiven us? Jesus once told a story to illustrate the consequences of failing to forgive.

The story is in Matthew 18:21–35. You'll want to read it for yourself, since we can't quote all the verses here. But let me summarize this familiar story.

It began with a good question. Peter asked Jesus, "Lord, how often shall my brother sin against me and I forgive him? Up to seven times?" (v. 21). Jesus' answer was "up to seventy times seven" (v. 22), and then He told the story of a king whose servants owed him some money.

The first servant owed the king the equivalent of ten to twelve million dollars, a staggering amount. The king ordered that he and his family be sold to pay the debt, but the slave begged for mercy. So the king forgave him the entire debt.

But this same slave went out and started choking another slave who owed him about one hundred dollars. When he couldn't pay, his cruel fellow servant had him tossed into prison.

Word of this got back to the king, and he was very angry. He called in the forgiven, but unforgiving, servant, and turned him over to the torturers until his huge debt was repaid.

This is usually understood to mean that the man was thrown into prison to be tortured until he could pay back the ten to twelve million. But I don't think that debt was the repayment issue here. Let me show you why.

First of all, how was the servant going to pay back such a huge amount of money in jail? He wouldn't even be able to work. Besides, the money had been forgiven earlier. I think the only debt the evil servant owed his king was to forgive the debt of his fellow servant who owed him a hundred dollars. Since he failed to do that, he had to suffer the negative consequences of his unforgiveness.

I believe this is what Jesus was teaching because He said at the end, "My heavenly Father will also do the same to you, if each of you does not forgive his brother from your heart" (v. 35).

This is the same principle announced in the Lord's Prayer: "Forgive us as we forgive others." If we fail to forgive others, God will hold us to the same harsh standard of unforgiveness we exacted against our brother or sister. God will reject fellowship with the believer who seeks relational forgiveness and yet is unwilling to grant it. This loss of fellowship with God is seen in many believers who constantly suffer from stress, depression, and discouragement.

But the positive consequences of forgiveness are awesome. They include peace of mind, restored relationships, and vital communion with God. In fact, the apostle James said that those who extend mercy to others receive mercy from God (James 2:13).

Therefore, don't destroy the bridge of forgiveness to others that you yourself must cross.

The Protection of Prayer

The last verse of the Lord's Prayer (Matthew 6:13) is the longest, and it's a very fitting way to end this great model prayer for Jesus' disciples. Let's take it phrase by phrase.

Jesus said we should pray, "And do not lead us into temptation, but deliver us from evil." This has presented a problem for many people. Why would we have to ask God not to lead us into temptation? Is that something He might do?

The point is not that God might lead us into something we shouldn't be doing and we have to pray that He won't. This is a request for divine protection in the midst of a fallen world that bombards us with evil all day every day.

From the time we wake up in the morning until we

go to bed at night—and even while we're sleeping—you and I are in spiritual danger. The entire system of this world and the demonic world is aligned against us. We'd better be asking our Father for protection from evil.

You need to understand that the Greek word translated "temptation" here is actually a neutral word. It can be used negatively, as in a temptation to do evil, or positively, as in a test the Lord sends our way to strengthen and mature us. We have to study the context to tell which meaning is in view.

If you go to the gym to lift weights and get in shape, you are under a heavy burden while you're lifting those weights. But it is a good burden because it is designed to tone and exercise your muscles. That's a positive use of weights.

But if somebody took a heavy weight and threw it at you to hurt you, that would definitely be a negative use of weights. If that weight hit you, you'd be in pain, even more than you're in pain when you're lifting. But the pain is different. It came from a different source, and had a different purpose—one to develop you and the other to harm you.

That's the difference between God's trials and the devil's temptations. God wants to develop us. Satan throws evil at us to destroy us. And the interesting thing is that sometimes the same event can be used by God for good and by the devil for evil (see Joseph's statement to his brothers in Genesis 50:20).

This is broken out quite nicely for us in James 1,

where James used the same word Jesus used in both of its meanings. First we see God's use of trials or tests to produce spiritual endurance in us and make us "perfect and complete, lacking in nothing" (James 1:2–4).

This is why Jesus told us to pray, "Your kingdom come. Your will be done." When you are committed to God's kingdom program, He can bring a tough circumstance, a real trial, across your path without your fretting about what you have done wrong or wondering why in the world you should have to endure something hard.

Instead, you know this is a trial to develop you because you know that "the testing of your faith produces endurance" (James 1:3). How do you know that? By faith. How do you get that kind of understanding? You ask God for it (v. 5).

You may be going through a big-time test right now. Let me give you some good news. The harder the test, the greater the spiritual growth. So if you are in a fire right now, you're getting ready for a hot blessing!

This is the positive use of trials. But James used this same word negatively when he said, "Let no one say when he is tempted, 'I am being tempted by God'; for God cannot be tempted by evil, and He Himself does not tempt anyone" (James 1:13).

James went on to say that if you are tempted and fall into sin, you do so on your own with an assist from the devil. These are the temptations from which we need God's protection so we don't fall into sin.

Understanding this should take some of the pressure off of us, because a lot of us are feeling guilty for the wrong thing. We feel guilty because our flesh wants to do wrong. We tell the flesh to stop feeling that way, but it doesn't work.

I have news for you. Your flesh, that old human nature still within you as a leftover from Adam, will always want to do wrong. It is corrupt, and it always will be until you die and your body becomes worm food. Paul said, "I know that nothing good dwells in me, that is, in my flesh" (Romans 7:18).

So don't feel bad when your flesh wants to do wrong. Remember that your old nature is not you. You've been given a new nature by Jesus Christ. Your flesh is merely the sin-contaminated tent that your new nature lives in temporarily.

Don't misunderstand. This does not mean we can indulge our flesh in sin on the excuse that we can't help it and our flesh isn't the real us anyway. Oh, no. We are under obligation to control and conquer our fleshly desires, and we can do that because we have the superabundant power of God available to us in the Holy Spirit.

The process of God's protection is described in 1 Corinthians 10:13. Paul wrote, "No temptation has overtaken you but such as is common to man; and God is faithful, who will not allow you to be tempted beyond what you are able, but with the temptation will provide the way of escape also, so that you will be able to endure it."

I like that word *overtaken* because it means you are

minding your own business, not out looking for trouble, when a temptation crosses your path. When that happens, you need to understand that God is faithful. You can count on Him to respond when you are tempted.

That means even the attacks of Satan that come your way are controlled by God. He only lets a certain number get through, and it's never more than you can bear.

Not only will God limit the extent of the temptation, He will provide an escape route. Notice the two little words "with" and "also" at the end of this verse. God will provide the escape route at the same time He allows the trial. The escape comes along with the temptation. They both show up at the same time.

This is important to understand because we are not in the habit of looking for the exit when we are being tempted. But if Satan puts you in a box, God cuts a hole in the box.

By the way, this same principle works even if we understand 1 Corinthians 10:13 to be talking about God-sent trials instead of the devil's temptations. No matter how hard or painful the trial, God promises that He will not allow it to take you under.

Of course, we would like this promise to say that God will provide us with an escape route so we can avoid trials altogether. But that's not the way the Christian life works.

So if you're being bombarded by temptation, pray that God will deliver you from evil. Ask Him to show you the way out, because it's there. And if you can't see the way out, ask God for the wisdom to find it (James 1:5).

When you pray, "Do not lead us into temptation, but deliver us from evil," you are saying, "Father, You know what I can handle today. Only give me what I can bear, and that which is going to help me. And deliver me from the Evil One."

The ultimate purpose of prayer is to praise and glorify the Lord.

Why should we pray for protection? Because we need it desperately, and because God is a delivering God. He delivered Esther and the Jewish people from annihilation in Persia. He delivered Daniel from the lion's den and Peter from prison. And even though Stephen was stoned to death, he looked up and saw heaven opened and Jesus waiting to receive him.

Even when it's time to die, God delivers you. The thief on the cross next to Jesus was in the worst shape possible, but Jesus promised him heaven that very day.

We pray for protection because God loves to deliver His people, so that His people may honor Him.

The Purpose of Prayer

We have come to the final section of the prayer Je-

41

sus gave us to teach us how to pray. The last request in the Lord's Prayer is "For Yours is the kingdom and the power and the glory forever. Amen" (Matthew 6:13).

Jesus teaches that when you finish praying, you are to offer God a doxology. The ultimate purpose of prayer is to praise and glorify the Lord.

Doxology is made up of two words that mean to praise and to speak or utter. So a doxology is an utterance of praise. But it's different from ordinary praise. A doxology is the kind of praise that erupts when a basketball player sinks the winning shot with one-tenth of a second left on the clock. Those points don't count any more than any of the other points in the game, but they're different from all those other points.

David broke out in praise at the offerings given for the building of the temple. As he contemplated the glory and greatness of God, David said,

> "Blessed are You, O Lord God of Israel our father, forever and ever. Yours, O Lord, is the greatness and the power and the glory and the victory and the majesty, indeed everything that is in the heavens and the earth; Yours is the dominion, O Lord, and You exalt Yourself as head over all." (1 Chronicles 29:10–11)

David was so overwhelmed with the presence of God that he couldn't keep it to himself. Something is wrong with the Christian who always holds it in and tries to keep the praise under wraps all the time. Every now and again, you need to let it out when the glory and the greatness and the marvel of God overwhelms you.

I love the way Paul let it all out in Romans 11:33–36. After talking about the glorious plan and program of God, Paul couldn't restrain his praise any longer, and he broke out in a doxology that begins, "Oh, the depth of the riches both of the wisdom and knowledge of God! How unsearchable are His judgments and unfathomable His ways!" (v. 33).

Sometimes we are too sophisticated and inhibited in our worship. I'm not suggesting we lose our dignity or sense of decorum. But when the glory of God erupts in our souls, we need to let it out in spontaneous, exuberant praise to Him. A doxology is like a volcano erupting when the pressure from within becomes too great to contain.

In the Lord's Prayer, Jesus gives us four things that a doxology will express about God and to God. I need to point out that it's dangerous to exegete a doxology, because that's not its purpose. But with that word of caution, let's take these last four glorious concepts one by one.

First, Jesus taught us to pray, "Yours is the kingdom" (Matthew 6:13). This is a declaration that every other kingdom will fall when it faces the kingdom of God.

Not too long ago, a sale of Elvis Presley memorabilia brought in more than five million dollars. Presley was called "the king," but that king is dead. His kingdom is now a museum. Our King is alive! Jesus Christ sits on the throne of heaven, and His kingdom will rule forever and ever. Our King is not for sale.

A second fact about our King and His kingdom that ought to elicit a doxology is His power. "Yours is the kingdom and the *power*" (italics added). God is not an impotent King. He can perform whatever He desires for the good of His kingdom.

God's kingdom is always matched by God's power, which is unlimited and self-generating. Paul said it best in the doxology of Ephesians 3:20–21: "Now to Him who is able to do exceeding abundantly beyond all that we ask or think, according to the power that works within us, to Him be the glory in the church and in Christ Jesus to all generations forever and ever. Amen."

Here's a third reason for praise. "Yours is the kingdom and the power and the *glory*" (italics added). The word *glory* means to be weighty or heavy. We used to say in the 1960s, "That dude is heavy." We meant the person was important in some way, someone worth paying attention to.

That's what glory means. When we give God glory, we are assigning to Him the significance that is due Him. God's glory is so surpassingly great that nothing else in the universe can compare to it.

If anything should call forth a doxology from you and me, it is God's glory. His glory was made visible in the Old Testament in the "shekinah" (see Ezekiel 43:1–5). God's invisible glory is made visible to us in another way when God suddenly moves in our lives and makes a way where there is no way.

Paul offered another doxology when he was discussing the greatness of God and the return of Jesus

Christ. The apostle referred to the Lord as "the blessed and only Sovereign, the King of kings and Lord of lords, who alone possesses immortality and dwells in unapproachable light; whom no man has seen or can see. To Him be glory and eternal dominion! Amen" (1 Timothy 6:15–16). "Unapproachable light" means God is brighter than the sun. We can't even approach the sun without getting cooked, yet the God who created the sun is infinitely brighter than the sun.

That's why God had to become a man to live among us. Jesus' glory had to be covered. What made the transfiguration (Matthew 17:1–9) so awesome and frightening for the disciples was that Jesus' humanity was opened for a moment and they saw the brilliant glory of deity.

The fourth concept Jesus gave us at the close of the Lord's Prayer is *forever.* We ought to praise God for His eternality. He has no beginning and no end.

Now if you think about this for too long and try to figure it out, you'll go mad. There has never been a time God has not been. That's why the best thing we can do is praise Him that He lives forever and that His kingdom will rule forever.

And don't miss the last word of the prayer, the *amen.* That's not just a nice word to tell everyone the prayer is over and they can raise their heads and relax. Amen means "Let it be, Lord. I agree with You. So be it. Even so, come Lord Jesus."

This is what it means to pray. We've covered a lot of ground and discussed a lot of crucial ideas. It's hard to adequately sum up a prayer like this in a few words, but let me try. Here's an "Evans paraphrase" of what we are saying to God when we pray as Jesus taught us to pray:

Lord, I acknowledge and bow before You, recognizing that You are my Father and the Father of all who believe. I know You live in heaven, and I want to give You the Honor You are due by hallowing Your name in everything I think, say, and do.

And because You are my heavenly Father, I will restructure my priorities so that I live for Your kingdom program, not my agenda. Let me get out my calendar and redo my schedule so that I can do Your will and not mine.

And Father, because I know who You are and where You live and how important Your kingdom program is, and because I have committed myself to live totally for Your kingdom and glory, I have several requests to make of You.

First, Lord, please give me the daily nutrients I need to have the energy to hallow Your name, serve Your kingdom, and do Your will.

And as I seek to hallow Your name, serve Your kingdom, and do Your will, forgive me for anything I've done to offend or fail You, even as You see that I have forgiven others who have done anything against me. Lord, I know that if I don't forgive others, You won't forgive me and my fellowship with You will be broken. Then You won't accept my praise and service.

Also, Father, as I go out to serve You today, don't let me get into something I can't handle. Don't give me a trial I can't deal with, because if I get into anything I can't deal with I'm going to embarrass Your name and Your kingdom.

And Lord, as I come to the end of my prayer, I want You to know that I understand this is not about me. I want You to know that I am so excited about worshiping Your Person, serving Your kingdom program, and accomplishing Your will on earth that I just can't contain my praise any longer.

Praise You for Your kingdom, which rules over all! Praise You for Your marvelous, incomparable power! Praise You for Your transcendent glory, which far outshines the sun! And praise You that it will be this way forever!

My friend, when you learn to pray like this and mean it, you are going to see heaven respond and earth shake. When you learn to pray like this, you are going to experience the power and glory and presence of God as never before.

The disciples said to Jesus, "Lord, teach us to pray" (Luke 11:1). Jesus did that, and now it is our privilege and lifelong challenge to learn to pray as Jesus has taught us to pray. Let our prayer also be, "Lord, teach us to pray." And then, let us pray!

THE URBAN ALTERNATIVE

The Philosophy

Dr. Tony Evans and TUA believe the answer to transforming our culture comes from the inside out and from the bottom up. We believe the core cause of the problems we face is a spiritual one; therefore, the only way to address them is spiritually. And that means the proclamation and application of biblical principles to the four areas of life—the individual, the family, the church, and the community. We've tried a political, social, economic, and even a religious agenda. It's time for a kingdom agenda.

The Purpose

We believe that when each biblical sphere of life functions properly, the net result is evangelism, discipleship, and community impact. As people learn how to govern themselves under God, they then transform the institutions of family, church, and government from a biblically based kingdom perspective.

The Programs

To achieve our goal we use a variety of strategies, methods, and resources for reaching and equipping as many people as possible.

- **Broadcast Media**
  The Urban Alternative reaches hundreds of thousands of people each day with a kingdom-based approach to life through its daily radio program, weekly television broadcast, and the Internet.

- **Leadership Training**
  Our national Church Development Conference, held annually, equips pastors and lay leaders to become agents of change. Teaching biblical methods of church ministry has helped congregations renew their sense of mission and expand their ministry impact.

- **Crusades/Conferences**
  Crusades are designed to bring churches together across racial, cultural, and denominational lines to win the lost. TUA also seeks to keep these churches together for ongoing fellowship and community impact. Conferences give Christians practical biblical insight on how to live victoriously in accordance with God's Word and His kingdom agenda in the four areas of life—personal, family, church, and community.

- **Resource Development**
  We are fostering lifelong learning partnerships with the people we serve by providing a variety of published materials. We offer books, audiotapes,

videos, and booklets to strengthen people in their walk with God and ministry to others.

- Project Turn-Around
  PTA is a comprehensive church-based community impact strategy. It addresses such areas as economic development, education, housing, health revitalization, family renewal and reconciliation. To model the success of the project, TUA invests in its own program locally. We also assist other churches in tailoring the model to meet the specific needs of their communities, while simultaneously addressing the spiritual and moral frame of reference.

* * *

For more information, a catalog of Dr. Tony Evans's ministry resources, and a complimentary copy of Dr. Evans's monthly devotional magazine,
call (800) 800-3222 or
write TUA at P.O. Box 4000, Dallas TX 75208.